THE THREE-STAGE MODEL
OF COURSE DESIGN

The Instructional Design Library

Volume 39

THE THREE-STAGE MODEL OF COURSE DESIGN

John F. Feldhusen

Purdue University

Danny G. Langdon

Series Editor

**Educational Technology Publications
Englewood Cliffs, New Jersey 07632**

ANGLE

Library of Congress Cataloging in Publication Data

Feldhusen, John Frederick, 1926-
   The three-stage model of course design.

   (The Instructional design library; v. 39)
   Bibliography: p.
   1. Lesson planning. 2. Education—Curricula.
I. Title. II. Series: Instructional design library; v. 39.
LB1027.F36   371.3   79-26576
ISBN 0-87778-159-1

Printed in the United States of America.

Library of Congress Catalog Card Number: 79-26576.

International Standard Book Number: 0-87778-159-1.

First Printing: March, 1980.

FOREWORD

The reader will come to appreciate the Three-Stage Model both for its simplicity and its effectiveness. This simplicity is found in the learning sequence suggested to promote learning of outcomes that are themselves often at complex levels. This design is of direct value in learning specific objectives, but it is the broader goals we often seek for our students—but elude our efforts—which are the main focus of attention. It appears that the years of effort put into formulating this design have paid off.

The basics of the design are well explained and illustrated. Also, the many surrounding, functional parts which support the design are described in full. These range from how to handle goals and objectives to the use of teacher aides for implementation and updating of course structure. The author has provided abundant guidance to prospective users of this design.

Danny G. Langdon
Series Editor

PREFACE

What is a good way to design a course so that (1) students will learn things you want them to learn, (2) students will enjoy their experiences in the course, (3) the instructor will enjoy designing and teaching the course, and (4) other instructors will view the course as a good model? The answer is probably that there are a number of ways to accomplish all four goals. That is what we set out to accomplish in designing the Purdue Three-Stage Model for instructional design.

Perhaps the most important issue in developing a model is the aesthetic one—do other instructors view or perceive it favorably? It seems likely that the promulgation of models has chiefly to do with the niceties of the parts and the organization of these parts. Moreover, those who try it out must find it a pleasant experience. Student learning and enjoyment are decidedly secondary concerns.

The new emphasis on technology in instructional development stresses empirical evaluation of an educational product or system as the *sine qua non*. We have evaluated student learning, student ratings, and instructor views, and we have concluded that the model is effective. Most of the research evaluation associated with the model has been conducted in the context of the undergraduate educational psychology courses at Purdue University.

I am deeply indebted to my colleagues, Russell E. Ames and Kathryn W. Linden, for their persistent efforts over the last five years in developing and testing the model in our educational psychology courses. Both are excellent teachers and instructional developers. Thus, it is likely that they would have great success in implementing any reasonable instructional model.

I am also indebted to many graduate students who have worked on various aspects of the model and its development. In particular, the innovative work of Kevin Hynes (now a Professor at the University of Nebraska) in cooperation with Professor William Richardson of Purdue University in implementing the model in vocational education at the high school level has been noteworthy.

Finally, I am indebted to William Kryspin (now a Professor at Governors State University) for the help he gave me when I first attempted to put the whole model together and implement it in an undergraduate educational psychology course.

A model is a heuristic device which should bring about both implementation and further creative development of the model itself. I hope that this document will inspire others not only to try the model in their own courses, but also to examine it carefully and bring about changes or additions which ultimately will make it a still better model for instructional design.

J.F.F.

CONTENTS

ABSTRACT

THE THREE-STAGE MODEL
OF COURSE DESIGN

This book is about the Purdue Three-Stage Model of course design. The model provides for information transmission to students, the development of higher level understanding of course material, and experience in applying concepts and principles to realistic situations.

A course of instruction is divided into six to eight units, each of which has some common theme or unity. For each unit, three instructional guides are developed. The first, called "self-instructional guide" (SIG), is a one-page document offering a one-paragraph introduction to the unit, a brief list of information-level objectives, a list of reading references and self-instructional materials, and a self-quiz. The student uses the guide to prepare for a mastery quiz.

After passing the mastery quiz, students are next given the "group instructional guide" (GIG) and organized into small groups for a learning project. The GIG, a one-page document, gives a brief introduction to the second stage of the unit, offers objectives at the comprehension and application levels, and specifies the task and product for the learning project. Students work in small groups of four to eight on a realistic problem using concepts and principles learned in stage one. Their product is graded on a pass-fail basis for the group.

In stage three of the unit, students receive a one-page

document called "procedures for individual projects" (PIP). It gives a brief introduction, states several application and synthesis objectives, and provides direction for an individual task in which students use their learning from stages one and two to solve a problem or do a project related to their own interests and/or to the professional field of their major area of study. The project results in a product which is graded on an A-B-C-D basis.

Closure activities at the end of a unit are used to help students organize their learning into a meaningful whole for the unit and to induce students to internalize their learning. Throughout a unit, the instructor serves as a resource person, coordinator, feedback source, and motivator. Students are required to take an active role in all aspects of the learning process as it proceeds through the three stages.

THE THREE-STAGE MODEL
OF COURSE DESIGN

I.

USE

Most courses follow a traditional design that has been used for hundreds of years. The instructor decides what topics will be "covered" in the course, often on the basis of topics which are presented in one or more of the available textbooks. More ambitious instructors include topics which are only treated in primary sources, such as articles, research reports, or specialized books. The really ambitious instructor prepares an outline of topics to be covered, sometimes in a sequence that even departs from the order of presentation in the available textbooks.

The outline is divided up according to the number of weeks of a term, semester, or special session. Students are told to read in the prescribed sources, and they may be given a list of supplementary readings on the course topics and urged to read as much as possible. While the students might be urged to read on a regular weekly schedule to be ready for the lectures or discussions each week, the real motivation to read will come in the form of the two or three scheduled hourly examinations.

Meanwhile, the instructor delivers lectures or conducts discussions from day to day related to the assigned topics and readings. In order to interpret the lectures properly or to participate meaningfully in discussion, the student should have—but rarely has—done the reading. Instead, the student takes notes furiously, hoping that the combination of notes now and reading later will eventually make sense and prepare him/her for the scheduled examination.

The examinations will either test the student's memory of a large number of separate pieces of information (the objective test) or his/her ability to write essays on larger chunks of information. Typically, there will be no specific preparation for the tests, just a transmission of information. That is, students will not have the opportunity to try out a variety of multiple-choice or essay test items on the course topics prior to tests. However, from test to test the student might become able to understand better what and how to study for succeeding tests.

This is the prevalent model for the design of instruction. But there are exceptions. There are courses in which there are specific skills to be learned, and the courses are designed to help students achieve those skills. This is often true of professional courses, such as speech therapy, clinical psychology, pharmacy, medicine, nursing, etc. There are also the exceptions generated by some of the new design models which have achieved at least modest popularity, such as the Personalized System of Instruction (PSI) or Keller Plan (Keller, 1968), Guided Design (Wales, 1973), or the Audio-Tutorial method (Postlethwait *et al.,* 1972).

Recognizing limitations in these newer models and being aware of the horrible failures of the traditional model, I set about designing a new approach to course design which would hopefully overcome some of the weaknesses and limitations of traditional courses and yet provide a defensible and practical approach to course design. The product is a model which my colleagues and I call the Purdue Three-Stage Model. The three stages are analogous to information input (stage one), development of understanding (stage two), and learning applications through internalization and transfer (stage three). The model is appropriate for use in all courses in which there is content which can be learned at a really meaningful level and which has applications in realistic professional and/or real-life activities.

Learning activities for a unit of instruction begin with information input activities (stage one). The instructor presents instructional objectives and learning activities designed to achieve the information. Usually, this means that the student proceeds to read or to use any of the various forms of self-instructional materials. Often there is a reliance on BOOK (*B*asic *O*rganization *O*f *K*nowledge) to achieve the information input. Typically, a student should be able to read or study the assigned material in one day or a few days. Then the student (as in PSI) takes a mastery test to determine if the information-level objectives have been achieved. Most students achieve this level rather easily.

Stage two is designed to carry the student to a level of understanding in which the information becomes meaningful. It typically involves small-group projects, simulations, or gaming activities. The latter are designed to encourage the student to begin to use simple information in meaningful and more complex project and problem-solving activities. Objectives are stated for this second stage which would typically fall at level two and higher of the Bloom *et al. Taxonomy* (1956). Students might spend two to eight hours in and out of class on a given group activity. It always involves a procedure (usually a written report) which is simply graded on a pass-fail basis. If the grade is fail, the group goes back to work.

Stage three is designed to provide opportunity for individual application and internalization of learning. The student is given general directions for a problem or project in which he/she will utilize information, skills, and concepts learned in stages one and two in designing a product or solving an appropriate problem. The student may meet with the instructor to clarify the exact nature of the project and to explore his/her own interests, which might be incorporated into the project. The individual project might take one or two days or as long as a week to complete. These projects are usually graded by the instructor on an A-B-C-D or point basis. The overall purpose of stage three is to facilitate transfer of material learned in stages one and two to realistic projects and problems which are of personal relevance for the student and which will meet his/her real-life needs.

From this description, it should be apparent that the three-stage model involves individualized instruction at stage one in the transmission or teaching of basic information. It also involves independent instructional activity in stage three in the individual projects. However, the model is nonprescriptive with regard to individualization of instruction. It might take the PSI form of personalized reading in a text under the control of specified objectives, or it might involve audio-tutorial units, or programmed instruction. In any event, *available* resources are the first choice in meeting instructional demands in stage one.

The three-stage model is clearly applicable to high school and college and university courses as well as to many other forms of adult education. Moreover, it seems unlikely that there are any inherent features which would even limit its use at the elementary level, except student ability to read and write quite well. A considerable amount of maturity may be necessary to provide motivation and capacity for self-direction in stages one and three.

The model is most clearly applicable in subject matter areas which provide opportunities for application to projects or problem-solving activities that involve a substantial information base to be learned at a meaningful level. It would probably have limited value in clinical, practicum, and motor skill courses.

One unexpected application of the model is in the area of workshops and short courses. It has been used as the guiding framework in the design of workshops as short as two hours or as long as a week. In these applications, the information input in stage one has been modified to include presentations or lectures to an entire group along with abbreviated handouts offering condensed information for individual study. The iterations of stages are handled in continuous fashion with no assumption of outside study by participants.

Experimentation and development of the three-stage model for the design of college courses began in 1971. All of the original work and much of the continued development have been in the subject matter of educational psychology. It is obvious that each of the three stages relates closely to a well-known instructional model. Stage one most closely resembles the Personalized System of Instruction (PSI) pioneered by Keller (1968). Stage two utilizes the small-group teaching system which has been described and reviewed recently by Sharan and Sharan (1976). Stage two may also involve gaming and simulation as vehicles for the small-group activity (Horn, 1977). Finally, stage three involves independent study and project activity, both well-developed instructional techniques.

The unique or innovative quality of the three-stage model lies, then, not in the instructional techniques used within stages, but rather in the integration and sequencing of the instructional activities in the three stages. The model stresses the importance of formulating both broad goals and specific instructional objectives throughout all three stages of activity, and the objectives are framed within the rubric of the Bloom *et al. Taxonomy* (1956). A number of other innovative instructional techniques are also employed in the system, and they will be described in a later section of this book.

The Purdue Three-Stage Model for design of courses is applicable to a wide range of subject matter, courses, and workshops. The developer's task is not as great as in some other systems because there is much utilization of instructional resources. The model seems to work well in small classes of as few as 15-20 students or in large classes of 70-80 students. Managing the operations of a course within this design probably involves some new skills not normally required in traditional courses. The payoffs for the instructor can be substantial in terms of student appreciation of the course, its "relevance," its overall motivational qualities, and the amount and quality of learning.

References

Bloom, B.S. *et al. Taxonomy of Educational Objectives, Handbook I: Cognitive Domain.* New York: Longman, Inc., 1956.

Horn, R.E. *The Guide to Simulations/Games for Education and Training.* Cranford, N.J.: Didactic Systems, 1977.

Keller, F.S. Goodbye, Teacher... *Journal of Applied Behavior Analysis,* 1968, *1,* 78-89.

Postlethwait, S.N., Novak, J., and Murray, H.T. *The Audio-Tutorial Approach to Learning.* Minneapolis: Burgess, 1972.

Sharan, S., and Sharan, Y. *Small-Group Teaching.* Englewood Cliffs, N.J.: Educational Technology Publications, 1976.

Wales, C.E. Programmed Instruction—Guided Design. *NSPI Newsletter,* 1973, *12,* 1-9.

II.

OPERATIONAL DESCRIPTION

This section will describe the operations of the Purdue Three-Stage Model as it might be experienced by a student or as viewed by an outside observer. The major topics to be covered include:

    (a) introduction and orientation to a course and its goals;

    (b) the self-instructional guide (SIG);

    (c) alternative modes of testing;

    (d) the group instructional guide (GIG) and group activities;

    (e) projects, tasks, simulations, games;

    (f) small-group dynamics;

    (g) grading of projects;

    (h) the procedures for individual projects (PIP);

    (i) evaluation of projects;

    (j) sequencing of a unit and overlap of units;

    (k) closure and internalization activities; and

    (l) teaching assistants.

Figure 1 presents a concise overview of the three-stage model. For each stage, the chart shows the major purpose, the levels of behavioral objectives addressed, illustrative objectives, the media or audio-visual materials used, the instructional methods appropriate to that stage, the role of the instructor, and the nature of the testing and evaluation.

Figure 1

The Three-Stage Model

	Major Purpose	Taxonomy Levels	Illustrative Objectives	Media	Method	Instructor Role	Testing and Evaluation
Stage III	Application of knowledge to real problems.	Simulation of real-life tasks, application, and Bloom Taxonomy Levels 3, 4, 5, 6.	Do library research on mineral discoveries. Write a short story about life in a gold mining camp.	As needed to simulate problems. Procedures for individual projects (PIP).	Individuals work on simulated problems.	1. Prepare simulation problem materials. 2. Model problem-solving and creative thinking. 3. Aid individual students. 4. Prepare procedures for individual projects (PIP).	Formal evaluation of plans, designs, or solutions developed by individuals.
Stage II	Development of higher cognitive abilities.	Bloom Taxonomy Levels 3, 4, 5, 6.	How did the discovery of gold in the West affect eastern cities? Organize a debate on how to control world population. Prepare a report on current pollution problems in our state.	Overhead, slides, films, TV, blackboard, texts. Group instructional guide (GIG).	Students work in small groups on simulation tasks and problems.	1. Interact with and assist groups as they work on tasks and problems. 2. Prepare group instructional guide (GIG).	Informal evaluation of students through direct ongoing interaction with provision for formative feedback on the spot as necessary. Evaluation of group products on pass-fail basis.
Stage I	Mastery of basic subject matter.	Bloom Taxonomy Levels 1 and 2.	List major parts of the circulatory system. What were the major land routes to California used by the pioneers? What were the major sites of gold?	Text, programmed instruction, audio-tutorial, drill devices. Self-instructional guide (SIG).	Individualized instruction.	1. Design self-instructional material. 2. Develop a learning center. 3. Design self-instructional guide (SIG).	Mastery tests, true-false, matching, completion, multiple-choice, or reaction papers.

The chart can serve as a valuable guide to the following operational description of the three-stage model.

Introduction and Orientation. Most students are familiar with and expect the traditional mode of instruction described at the beginning of this book. Some even stubbornly *prefer* it and experience malaise in a new, innovative approach to instruction. Many students are also upset initially by a course format which seems to require a more active role for the student. The passivity of their role in traditional instruction is comforting to some students. Thus, there is a need at the outset of a course to tell the students about the alternative approach to be used in this course and even to argue for its superiority over traditional instruction. Hopefully, such an introduction and orientation will pave the way to greater student acceptance, success in learning, and even enthusiasm for the mode of learning and the subject matter.

The first step is to present a course syllabus and a description of the instructional model to all students. The syllabus is a statement of course procedures, requirements, and policies. It states the broad goals of the course (usually there are about seven to 12); the way SIGs (self-instructional guides), GIGs (group instructional guides), and PIPs (procedures for individual projects) will be used; the sequence and timing of course activities; testing and grading practices; attendance requirements; the role of the instructor and the TAs; and the instructor's general educational philosophy. Students are asked to read the syllabus before the second class meeting and to be prepared to ask questions at the second meeting.

The syllabus paves the way to student acceptance and understanding of the instructional system, but a continuing effort is needed for several weeks to help students understand the system and how to operate in it. It seems likely that this initial orienting activity is crucial in facilitating student acceptance and success in learning. Of course, such student orientation is probably vital in all new and complex instructional systems which depart from the traditional mode.

The Self-Instructional Guide (SIG). Each unit of instruction in a course will include one to three weeks of work. Each unit may involve a SIG, GIG, and a PIP and the associated activities of each. Typical units in an educational psychology course include (a) learning theories, (b) cognitive learning and outcomes, (c) motor learning, (d) social learning, (e) affective processes and objectives, (f) discipline and classroom management, (g) formulating objectives, and (h) testing.

The SIG is presented to students the first day of a new unit. An illustration is given in Figure 2. A SIG is typically a one-page statement which includes (a) the unit title, (b) a one-paragraph orienting introduction to the unit topic, (c) a statement of instructional objectives (usually at levels one and two of the Bloom *et al. Taxonomy* 1956), (d) a list of readings and/or self-instructional materials to be used (often the list offers several alternatives from which the student can make selections), and (e) some self-quizzing questions which the student can use to prepare for the quiz. The instructor may also give the class a brief oral introduction to the unit along with guidance concerning the instructional material, how to find and use it, etc. The self-instructional units are usually made available at a learning center, and special books or articles are accessed at a library reserve book room. The student proceeds to read and study for the mastery quiz.

Alternative Modes of Testing. For undergraduate classes, some form of mastery quizzing should be used. In preparation for the quiz, students are usually given two to five days to study the assigned material. At the next class meeting, after presentation of the SIG and after students have studied the assigned material, a mastery quiz is administered to the

---

Figure 2

SIG
(Self-Instructional Guide)
Goals of Instruction

Introduction

In this first unit, we want you to think seriously about and identify the broad goals which guide our efforts in teaching. They are perhaps the most important aspect of instruction. If we don't think about them, we slavishly commit ourselves to traditional procedures which may not really be commensurate with our own true values. The question is this: What are we trying to accomplish in our courses?

Objectives
(1) To be able to analyze a current ongoing course of instruction and identify the goals which seem to be guiding the effort.
(2) To be able to formulate a defensible set of goals based upon student and societal needs and our own value systems as instructors.
(3) To be able to translate those goals into specific objectives and procedures of instruction.

Instructional Activities
(1) Seek out and read some broad educational goal statements in your discipline.
(2) Read the paper "A Logical Approach to Curriculum Development."
(3) Read the paper "The Purdue Three-Stage Model."
(4) Write brief (one-two pages) reactions to each paper.

Self-Quiz
(1) How do goals differ from instructional objectives?
(2) How do values influence the selection of goals?
(3) Is it necessary to formulate objectives for all goals?
(4) Identify several major goals of courses in your area which are essentially subject matter goals.

---

class as a group, scored immediately, and feedback is provided in written form for each item missed. Students who fail to achieve the mastery criterion level must make an appointment to retake the quiz within a few days and after further study. Retesting is all done individually or in small groups by teaching assistants.

As an alternative, the PSI approach can be used, in which the mastery quizzes are given outside class time at a testing center staffed by teaching assistants. This approach presents logistical problems for some instructors, but it offers a great saving in the use of class time.

Another alternative which has been employed in graduate classes in which the three-stage model is used is to abandon quizzing altogether and to use what we call "Reaction Papers." In this format, students are told to read the assigned material for key or major ideas, to present these ideas in narrative form in the reaction paper, to suggest possible uses or implementation of the ideas, or to think of interpretive uses of the ideas in relation to other learning experiences. Such papers, usually four to eight pages long, lead to active reading and acquisition of major ideas. Students are also advised to use the objectives, stated in the SIG, as a guide in reading and writing the reaction paper.

The Group Instructional Guide (GIG). In the latter portion of the class session in which the mastery quizzing is carried out, the second stage group instructional activity is introduced, and small groups of four to seven students each are organized. The subsequent activities are guided by the group instructional guide (GIG), the instructor, and the teaching assistants. The ideal classroom is one in which students in each group can gather around a banquet-sized table. Minimally, they must have movable chairs, preferably at least with a writing arm.

Projects, Tasks, Games. The GIG looks much like a SIG. It is illustrated in Figure 3. It begins with an introductory

Figure 3

GIG
(Group Instructional Guide)
Goals of Instruction

Introduction

Goals of instruction derive from our philosophies, our values, our beliefs, our knowledge of our disciplines, our knowledge of instructional theory, our knowledge of students, and our biases.

We can do a better job of defining our goals by interacting with other people. We can learn about their goals and they can react to ours.

Objectives
(1) To be able to work with others in defining a set of instructional goals for a course at a specified level (e.g., freshman, sophomore, etc.).

(2) To be able to identify those goals which cut across disciplines.

Instructional Activities (Tasks and Products)
Work with your group to define a set of goals which might be used as instructional guides in courses which the several of you are teaching. If some goals are incompatible across your disciplines, identify them as such and indicate who espouses them.

paragraph which should serve as an introduction and organizer for this stage of activity. Then some instructional objectives are listed. They are typically at levels three to six of the Bloom *et al. Taxonomy* (1956), reflecting higher level cognitive goals. Finally, there is a statement of the group's task, how to go about and carry it out, and the product (usually a report) to be delivered. After a decade of explorations of the use of small groups in teaching, we concluded that unstructured discussions of texts and lectures or discussions guided by questions prepared by the instructor were of limited instructional value. Thus, a task-oriented approach to small-group activities was devised in which students must do a project, conduct a study, prepare a report, play a game, solve a problem, or participate in a simulation, all of which are designed to utilize information learned in stage one. Hopefully, the activities of stage two will carry the students to more meaningful or higher cognitive levels of learning.

Group Dynamics. These stage two projects are initiated in a class session and continued in the next two or three class sessions and outside of class by each group's own arrangements. Groups are urged to use a rotating leadership in their project work. The instructor and the TAs circulate among groups observing their progress and trying to determine if they are proceeding correctly. If they observe any troubles, they intervene and try to help the group clarify its direction. They serve as information resources to answer questions groups might have.

Grading the Project. The group product, report, or solution usually is in written form, but occasionally time is taken to have groups present an oral report to the whole class. The product is evaluated by the instructor on a pass-fail basis, and the members of each group share equally in the evaluation results. Several instructors have tried assigning letter grades or differential point values to the group product, but they have found that this often leads to disputes in a group concerning the relative input or failure of different group members. The pass-fail grading has eliminated this problem.

This group activity is highly productive in helping group members learn from one another. It is also productive in the learning that is evoked by the task experience. Further, the group project helps students learn how to cooperate with others and how to lead a group.

Procedures for Individual Projects (PIP). The third stage of the model involves the student in an individual application of the information and skills learned in stages one and two. The document distributed to students is illustrated in Figure 4. Like the SIG and the GIG, it begins with a one-paragraph introduction, which now stresses the application or use of the ideas learned in stages one and two. Next, some objectives are stated which focus on application of the material to real projects and problems. Then the task is presented. The student is encouraged to meet with the instructor to discuss his/her specific project and to clarify any issues which may be in doubt. The work on the individual project is then carried out by the student on his/her own time. At this same time, the instructor may begin the SIG for the next unit.

Evaluation of Projects. The individual projects always yield a product, often a narrative report, which is turned in and evaluated by the instructor. Letter grades or a point system are used. The evaluation of these projects constitutes the major evaluation component of the student's final grade.

Sequencing and Overlap of Units. The sequence of events in a unit of instruction may be conditioned by the typical temporal organization of a course. Most of the work at Purdue has involved three time patterns: (a) a course meeting three times a week, say Monday-Wednesday-Friday, for 50 minutes each class session; (b) a course meeting twice a week for 75-minute sessions; or (c) once a week for 150 minutes. The model is quite adaptable to all three situations.

Figure 4

PIP
(Procedures for Individual Projects)
Goals of Instruction

Introduction
Much teaching is mindless, thoughtless following of traditions. Many instructors fail to identify the broad goals which are really directing their teaching efforts. It seems likely that sound procedures for instructional development demand that we begin by examining our broad goals. All too often we begin by looking for a new technique or by embracing someone else's model of instruction. Let us begin by thinking for ourselves.

Objectives
(1) To be able to analyze a current, ongoing course of instruction and identify the goals which seem to be guiding the effort.
(2) To be able to formulate a defensible set of goals based upon student and societal needs, conditions of the discipline, and our own value systems.
(3) To be able to use the goals as guides in formulating objectives and designing instruction.

Tasks and Products
(1) Analyze one of the courses you are currently teaching and identify the broad goals which seem to underlie the course.
(2) Identify other goals which you believe should be pursued in your course(s).
(3) Use professional literature or guides from your own discipline in identifying broad goals.
(4) Prepare a statement as follows:
  (a) Goals already incorporated in the course design.
  (b) New goals which I hope to incorporate into the course.

In a situation involving three meetings per week, the events might be as follows. At the first meeting, the instructor distributes the SIG, gives a brief oral introduction to the new unit, and conducts some closing activities for the previous unit. At the next meeting, two or three days later, the mastery quiz is administered. If the assigned readings are lengthy, the mastery quiz would not be given until the second meeting after distribution of the SIG, when four or five days would have elapsed. For the intervening class session, students might be excused for study, or the time might be used for culminating activity of the previous unit. The quiz is then administered in class and scored immediately, or the students might go individually to a testing center as described earlier. In either situation, written feedback is offered after test scoring.

If the student fails the mastery quiz, he/she immediately makes an appointment for retesting. At this same class session, the GIG is then distributed, groups are organized, there is introductory discussion of the group project, and a date is set for completion of the task. In some units, the task requires that the members of a group have some commonality of background. If this is the case, the initial organization of groups involves such considerations. The next class meeting is then devoted to the group activity, with the instructor and TAs circulating and providing help and direction as necessary. Groups are also urged to meet on their own time at a place of their convenience. On the due date, groups submit their project or report, and then the PIP is delivered to all students. After some discussion of the requirements of the PIP, students may be dismissed. However, they are advised to see the instructor about their individual plans. At this same meeting, the SIG for the next unit may be distributed and discussed.

The individual project always involves some kind of application based on stage one and stage two learning and always permits much individualization to the student's needs, interests, and abilities. The project is typically due within a week. At the class meeting when the project is turned in, the instructor may conduct a closure discussion and seek student evaluation of the unit. Figure 5 gives an illustration of such a closure-evaluation instrument. At this point, the student should be about ready for the mastery quiz on the next unit.

The above sequence is easily adaptable to the format of a class which meets twice a week. However, substantial adaptations are needed when the class meets only once a week. This is often the case for graduate classes. In such cases, the following plan can be followed. At the end of a two and one-half hour class, the SIG for the next unit is distributed and discussed. Students are required to read and/or do the assigned books and minicourses and to write a reaction paper. As noted earlier, the reaction paper requires the student to identify major ideas or concepts and to discuss them in relation to his/her own background, needs, or interests. The reaction paper is collected at the beginning of the next session, and a general class discussion is held on the content. Then the GIG is distributed and the group activity for the evening is carried on. In graduate classes, this often culminates in an oral report, including overhead projection of parts of the product from each group. The evening then ends with the presentation of the PIP and discussion of the requirements of the individual project. In graduate classes, students are given the option of omitting some of the PIPs and selecting those in which they have the greatest need or interest. The SIG for the next unit is also presented. Then the session ends.

Closure Activities. In both graduate and undergraduate classes, instructors use some closure and evaluation activities at the end of most units. This may consist of a brief lecture by the instructor restating the goals of the unit and student accomplishments as he/she sees them. Students are also

Figure 5

Stage Three—Closure

Directions: Circle the letter of your choice and respond to questions.

1.   How much did you learn from the readings and self-instructional things listed on the SIG?
    A.   A great deal, accomplished objectives
    B.   A moderate amount, but could have learned more
    C.   Little or nothing
2.   If you circled B or C for number (1), what failures in you or the material could be blamed?

3.   How much did you learn from the group project (GIG)?
    A.   A great deal, accomplished objectives
    B.   A moderate amount, but could have learned more
    C.   Little or nothing
4.   If you circled B or C for number (3), what failures in you or the material could be blamed?

5.   How much did you learn from the individual project (PIP)?
    A.   A great deal, accomplished objectives
    B.   A moderate amount, but could have learned more
    C.   Little or nothing
6.   If you circled B or C for number (5), what failures in you or the material could be blamed?

7.   Which activity in this unit seems most related or connected to things you are learning in other courses?

8.   Which activities in this unit *seem* most relevant or useful to you in your future role as a teacher, counselor, therapist, or school administrator?

9.   In what ways, if any, have you clarified your views of yourself as a future teacher? Do you see your abilities, attitudes, or values in any new ways?

10.   What remains unclear, unanswered, uncertain in the content of this unit?

invited to comment on what they have gained, how they have related the work to their own special field and interests, and their evaluation of the unit.

Teaching Assistants (TAs). Early in the development of the three-stage model, it was obvious that developing, managing, and sustaining a course in this model with 35 or more students per class group placed great demands upon the instructor's time. A few graduate assistants were available to help instructors, but even their assistance was not enough. Thus, an undergraduate teaching assistant program was developed. Students who have completed one of our courses with a grade of A and who have performed well in all the course activities, as perceived by the instructors and the TAs, are invited to apply for assignment as undergraduate TAs for the subsequent or later semesters. A committee of faculty makes the final selection. One or two of these TAs is then assigned to each class of 30 or more students. Prior to their beginning work, they are given several hours of orientation, and they meet each week during the course with the instructor to aid in course planning. The TAs participate in all aspects of course management and development, including test development, test administration, assisting in small-group activities, and designing SIGs, GIGs, and PIPs. The TAs are given academic credit under a special practicum course number in the Education Department. Financial stipends have also been awarded to TAs for their services in some years, and this approach seems to be equally effective in motivating TAs to perform well.

Summary. In operation, the three-stage model affords an approach to course design which can be varied to suit the special inclinations of the instructor and the subject matter. The instructor's task of developing the course calls for extra, but not "back breaking," effort. Many of the basic instructional resources are drawn from available sources. At stage one, books, minicourses, and other self-instructional materials are the major vehicles of instruction. Often, the mastery quiz items can be drawn from existing test item files. At stage two, tasks or problems must be designed, and this can require substantial extra effort. However, it is also common to use games and simulations as the group activity in stage two, and these can often be drawn from published sources (Horn, 1977). In stage three, the instructor's task is to design the framework for an individualized student project. This is often not very difficult.

Additional illustrative units, each including a SIG, GIG, and PIP, are presented in Appendices A, B, C, and D. They represent units on The Nature of Giftedness and Talent, Instructional Objectives, Instructional Materials, and Testing. Thus, they provide examples in relatively divergent areas of instruction.

The instructor ultimately faces the task of orchestrating or managing the course with 30 or more students and two or three assistants. In practice, there are many possible variations of the model. Sometimes a unit ends after stage two because the instructor decides that there has been sufficient and adequate learning to obviate the need for stage three. Similarly, stage two is sometimes eliminated and students proceed from stage one directly to the individual projects. Some supplementary units have also been developed which only include the stage one activities of acquiring basic information. Ultimately, the model should be viewed as a heuristic device intended to generate rational approaches to course design.

References

Bloom, B.S. *et al. Taxonomy of Educational Objectives, Handbook I: Cognitive Domain.* New York: Longman, Inc., 1956.

Horn, R.E. *The Guide to Simulations/Games for Education and Training.* Cranford, N.J.: Didactic Systems, 1977.

III.

DESIGN FORMAT

The major goal of the three-stage model for design of courses is to provide a context within which meaningful and relevant student learning can occur. Viewed from the standpoint of the Bloom *et al. Taxonomy* (1956), this means that a major purpose is to help students go beyond the usual level one learning of rote information and to achieve comprehension, ability to analyze and synthesize, and capacity to evaluate or exercise intelligent judgment. This is a big order, to be sure. But such purposes are rarely achieved, if no special effort is made.

In this section of the book, the major components and characteristics of the three-stage model will be presented in depth. The point of view is now the instructor's. How does he/she go about the creation of a new course in this model? To answer the question, the following set of specific sub-problems will be discussed:

    (a) formulating broad goals and specific objectives;

    (b) designing SIGs;

    (c) designing GIGs;

    (d) designing PIPs;

    (e) closure and internalization activities;

    (f) selecting and training TAs;

    (g) recordkeeping and grading;

    (h) the course syllabus and outline; and

    (i) the roles of instructors and TAs.

Formulating Goals and Objectives. Charles Silberman, in his book *Crisis in the Classroom* (1970), argued that a major problem in all teaching and instructional development is that people do not think about the major goals of their effort.

> What is mostly wrong with colleges and universities is mindlessness. (p. 36)

He went on to say:

> At the heart of this problem is the failure to think seriously about purpose or consequence. It is the failure at every level to ask *why* we are doing what we are doing or to inquire into the consequences. (p. 36)

Goals are the broad statements of aims or consequences that reflect *serious thought* about purposes of education. Goals can be mindless or ineffectual, as witness the items which appear in many college and university catalogs:

- well-rounded citizenship;
- appreciation of the arts;
- mental health; or
- occupational competence.

These goals are too broad to have any effective meaning in designing instruction.

In contrast, the following set of goals is the result of careful thought about purposes for a course:

- know the scientific method;
- develop a sense of social responsibility;
- know basic concepts and principles;
- develop ability to analyze and solve real problems;
- develop skill in evaluating decisions; or
- prepare plans for operating systems.

In contrast to the first list, the second is a carefully planned set of goals. The group of people who developed these goals have taken themselves seriously in developing a course of instruction.

Here are some other goals suggested by people from various disciplines:

- develop favorable attitudes;
- self-discipline;
- respect for other points of view;
- creative problem-solving; or
- learn the role of a professional.

The following additional illustrative goals are cited from Robert Mager's book, *Goal Analysis* (1972):

- develops an awareness of civic responsibility;
- appreciates good literature;
- understands environmental needs;
- uses safety procedures;
- develops initiative; or
- able to ask relevant questions.

But goals are "fuzzies," Mager says. They have to be translated into instructional objectives. Objectives are the specifications for what students will be able to do if teaching is successful. They are the curriculum. They are invaluable in designing instruction. They are indispensable in developing tests or evaluation procedures.

Objectives which relate to subject matter—to the learning of information, concepts, and principles—should be carefully thought out to make sure that all appropriate levels of the higher cognitive processes are included. Instructors should outline content or subject matter to be taught before they write objectives to be sure that all items which should be covered are included, that dead knowledge is excluded, and that relationships between items of content have been carefully thought out. This is also a good stage for professors to be working together in order to argue out what should not be taught and what the meaning of concepts or principles to be taught really is. The *Taxonomy of Educational Objectives, Handbook I: Cognitive Domain* (Bloom *et al.,* 1956) can serve as a guide to formulating objectives from the low level of small pieces of information up through judgment or decision-making. Here is a brief form of the *Taxonomy.*

- Level 1. *Knowledge or information.*

  Memorizable units, chunks, or sequences of information.
- Level 2. *Comprehension.*

  To know concepts and principles with appropriate meaning.
- Level 3. *Application.*

  Ability to use concepts and principles in solving problems.
- Level 4. *Analysis.*

  Ability to identify elements or parts and their interrelationships.
- Level 5. *Synthesis.*

  Ability to develop plans, systems, or approaches for real-world needs.
- Level 6. *Evaluation.*

  Ability to use standards or criteria in making judgments.

For the three-stage model as applied in an educational psychology course, the following goals have been formulated:

(1) learn a set of basic concepts, principles, and theories;

(2) develop higher cognitive abilities;

(3) learn how to apply knowledge to realistic professional problems;

(4) become self-directed learners;

(5) appreciate the course as a model of instructional design;

(6) experience personal relevance in the course experiences;

(7) develop competence in working with others on professional problems; and

(8) learn to help one another achieve course goals.

These goals are communicated to students at the beginning of the course as part of a short description of the overall course design. They serve as the overriding basis for all subsequent course design.

As noted earlier and illustrated in Figures 2, 3, and 4, specific instructional objectives are written for the SIGs, GIGs, and PIPs. For the SIG at stage one, the objectives are generally at levels one and two of the Bloom *Taxonomy*:

- List the basic steps in developing a behavioral management program for a classroom discipline problem. (level one, knowledge)
- Give several illustrations of the concept of behavioral shaping. (level two, comprehension)

The basic purpose of stage one instruction is to teach subject matter or transmit information at a meaningful level.

The statement of objectives for a GIG for the group activity is typically at levels three to six of the *Taxonomy*:

- Using the concepts of "threats to internal validity," analyze a proposed research design and identify its weaknesses. (level three, application)
- Examine the instructional system and identify its major components. (level four, analysis)
- Design a grading system based on principles of evaluation. (level five, synthesis)
- Evaluate three instructional systems using criteria of motivational power, cost efficiency, and student achievement. (level six, evaluation)

At stage three, the PIP includes another statement of objectives, which is most likely to be at level five of the *Taxonomy*. The objectives may also stress incorporation of the student's own needs and interests in the activity.

The objectives stated in the SIG, GIG, and PIP supplement the directions for carrying out the tasks and developing products. In effect, they tell the student how to carry out the assignment. Thus, if a student is working on a PIP project to design a behavioral management system, the objectives in the SIG, GIG, and PIP which relate to contingencies, shaping, and successive approximations tell him/her that these are probably elements of the system.

The statements of objectives provide focus and direction for each of the three stages, they delimit the tasks at stages two and three, and they provide specifications for evaluation of student progress.

Designing SIGs. The self-instructional guides have four major parts: introduction, objectives, a list of learning resources, and a self-quiz. Of course, the title for the unit and the identification as a SIG or self-instructional guide appear at the top. For most of the units, a one-page format is used. The introduction should serve two purposes: (1) as an advance organizer (Ausubel, 1968), and (2) as a motivator to develop the student's interest in the unit. Here is an illustration of an introduction for a SIG in a unit on learning theories:

> In this unit, we will be studying learning theories. Learning theories help us in two ways. First, they help us understand how students learn and why they sometimes fail to learn. Thus, some of our perplexing problems of teaching can be clarified. Secondly, and much more importantly, theories offer us principles and guidelines for designing instruction. They can tell how to plan our teaching of a unit. Hopefully, they will help us do a better job of teaching. In this unit, we will learn about several theories which cover many aspects of classroom instruction.

The first four sentences serve as organizers, providing an overview of the unit. Motivation is induced by the statements of how students will benefit from the unit.

The next part of the SIG is the statement of the objectives. They should provide further orientation and guidance as the students go about their study. Here are the objectives for the unit on learning theories:

(a) identify the basic components of each of several theories;

(b) explain how motivation functions within each theory; and

(c) describe memoric processes in each theory.

The next part of the SIG lists the learning resources. This might include books, articles, self-instructional minicourses, computer-assisted instruction, films, videocassettes, etc. It is preferable to offer alternatives and to afford students the chance to use several resources. Here are the resources, as listed, for the unit on learning theories:

(a) *Learning and Human Abilities,* 4th Edition, Chapter 2;

(b) *Psychology for Teaching,* Chapters 4, 7, 14;

(c) *Theories of Learning,* Chapters 5, 12, 14;

(d) *Learning Theories for Teachers,* 3rd Edition, Chapters 5, 7, 8; and

(e) The Minicourse on "Learning Theories."

The final part of the SIG is the self-quiz. This usually includes several discussion or listing questions which are closely tied to the objectives. The following are illustrative questions for the learning theories unit:

(a) What components of the three theories are common to two or three of the theories?

(b) How would you explain the motivational problem, within each theory, of a child who shows no interest in a teaching unit on butterflies?

(c) Which of the theories seems to offer the best explanation of memory processes? Why?

The last question calls for inferential and judgmental activity beyond levels one or two, but it should nevertheless evoke levels one and two processing cognitions in support of learning.

The design of SIGs calls for skill in writing and formulating objectives. It is also advantageous to have a broad grasp or experience with instructional resources. SIGs can be modified easily from semester to semester in light of student successes and failures in using them.

The SIG prepares students for the mastery quiz on the

unit. Mastery quizzes for each unit should be chiefly in objective test form. This might include multiple-choice, true-false, matching, and completion or short-answer items. Ideally, a test item file should be developed with enough items for each unit to cover the needs for several alternate quiz forms of 15 to 20 items each. As they are used, the test items should be analyzed for discrimination and difficulty, and the information should be recorded on the test item file cards. Figure 6 gives an illustration of a card used in a test item file.

It should be noted that, since the testing within this model is on a mastery basis, the usual item statistics must be evaluated differently from norm-referenced tests. If the mastery level for overall quiz performance is set at 80 percent, it is reasonable to conclude that most good items will have difficulty levels at 80 percent and higher. It is also the case then that the discrimination power of items, in the norm-referenced sense, is inevitably lowered. This problem is discussed in the book *Developing Classroom Tests,* by Kryspin and Feldhusen (1974, p. 163).

Two different approaches to quiz administration have been used. One is to administer it the first time to an entire class on a specified day and to score it in class as each student finishes. Undergraduate and graduate teaching assistants (TAs) can assist in this testing process. After tests are scored, students receive a feedback sheet which gives text references for each test item. Students who fail to achieve the mastery level must make an appointment for retesting in a few days. As an alternative, in some courses, students are allowed to come individually for testing but with the proviso that they must come on or before some specified date. In this situation, alternate quiz forms are used to avoid communication of items from student to student, or a system, devised by Santogrossi and Roberts (1978), in which random sets of items are generated, is used. In this arrangement, the file of

Figure 6

A Test Item File Card

Item Type: Multiple-choice	Topic: Child development	Objective: Able to identify Piagetian stages	Reference: Phillips Text
Item: Which stage of development is characterized by strong egocentrism? A. sensorimotor B. preoperational C. concrete operations D. formal operations			
Item Performance Data: • Date administered — Oct., 1977 • Number of students — 67 • Difficulty — .71 • Discrimination — .53			

items for a unit is on cards. As each student arrives, he/she or the proctor draws ten items randomly. The student then takes the cards and writes responses on an answer sheet. When finished, he/she presents the cards and the answer sheet to the proctor, who uses the code number on the cards to refer to a key and to score the quiz quickly. The student learns the results immediately. If the student fails, immediate counseling is available from the proctor, with guidance on how to study for a retake of the quiz a day or so later.

The criterion performance level on quizzes should be kept at a reasonable level, which assures adequate performance at stages two and three. Excessively high levels of performance, requiring mastery of great detail, can rarely be justified. Thus, an 80 percent level is usually satisfactory.

Mastery testing seems to be an appropriate approach to motivating students to study assigned material and to evaluate the effectiveness of their study at the undergraduate level. Its success as a motivational and evaluative technique is well demonstrated in PSI courses. However, as students achieve greater maturity in their junior and senior years and as graduate students, alternative modes of motivation and evaluation seem more appropriate. Thus, an alternative, the "reaction paper" system, has been developed.

The reaction paper is a narrative report in which a student demonstrates that he/she has identified major concepts and principles in the assigned readings. It is also an effort to induce creativity and application in the student's study. Students are encouraged to speculate about potential application of ideas, relate new concepts to their own previous experiences, and evaluate new concepts in relation to specified criteria.

While some effort is made in the course syllabus and in each SIG to spell out the demands of the reaction paper, many students require several iterations of trial writing and instructor feedback to "get the idea." Here are the directions used in the syllabus in a graduate course:

As you read assigned material for each SIG, note the salient concepts and principles which are presented. Don't worry about minute details. When you finish reading, begin writing your reaction paper. State one of the major ideas. Restate its meaning for you. How might *you* use or apply the idea? How does it relate to some aspects of your own experience or things you have learned previously? Is it a sound idea? One big paragraph should do it.

Don't list ideas in the reaction paper. Don't critique or simply tear ideas apart. Don't outline. Try to be creative and informal in developing your ideas.

Grading of reaction papers has usually been on a pass-fail basis. This has made it possible for instructors to read the papers rapidly and to offer minimum feedback except to students who have difficulty in writing reaction papers. Instructors are encouraged to write several sentences of comment on each paper overall and to comment briefly on papers throughout the text to provide evidence to students that the instructor is indeed reading the whole paper.

The experience of instructors with reaction papers, as an alternative to mastery testing, has been generally positive. However, some seniors and graduate students are weak in writing skills and have difficulty with reaction papers. These weaknesses include the inability to develop and elaborate a paragraph, incomplete sentences, faulty usage, awkward construction, etc.

The reaction paper serves well to motivate students to read assigned material carefully, to identify key ideas, and to think about potential applications. As a side benefit, the reaction paper probably helps students develop their creative writing abilities.

Designing GIGs. Group instructional guides (GIGs) are the guiding mechanism for the second stage of activities for a unit. The group activity is built upon information and concepts learned in stage one. This information is prerequisite to applications, analyses, syntheses, and evaluation activities carried out in the group activity.

The ideal small group has four to seven students seated around a small table. In some group projects, they may have to have similar backgrounds, but in others they can be mixed. The following GIG task illustrates a situation where a common background is desirable. The setting is an educational psychology course:

> Assume that you are a group of teachers who have been asked to develop a new introductory course in your field of teaching. Formulate a set of broad goals for this course. Identify which goals are clearly related to subject matter and which relate to other aspects of the course.

It is clear from this illustration that the group members should have a common subject-matter background. However, in the following illustration, such would not be the case.

> Analyze the typical public school classroom and its mode of operation. What aspects facilitate learning, which inhibit learning, in the light of principles of learning we have studied?

The introduction to the GIG should set the stage for the group activity by relating it to real-world applications. Here is an illustration:

> In this unit, you are learning how students' self-concepts develop in school. Much of that development has its roots in earlier experiences in school, at home, and in play with other children. Thus, in considering how current school activities and things the teacher does influence the self-concept, it is necessary to consider the interplay with the past experiences. In this group activity, you will analyze a classroom situation and its impact on a child with specified background experiences.

The objectives then build upon this introduction and give specific guidance to the student:

(1) be able to identify significant influences on self-concept in a given case situation;

(2) be able to evaluate the impact of current classroom experiences; and

(3) be able to suggest ways to modify current classroom practices to facilitate positive development of the self-concept.

The task and products should be clearly specified. There seems to be little difficulty in motivating students in small-group activities unless the task is vague and aimless. The following directions did not succeed in promoting an effective discussion:

> In your small group, discuss the ethical issues involved in behavior modification as used in the classroom.

An alternative which was successful was stated as follows:

> In your small group, identify at least five ethical issues involved in classroom use of behavior modification. State each in a brief paragraph. Then, for each issue, suggest a counter argument or a way of resolving the issue. Your group report should be typed if possible, proofread by all the group members, and turned in to your instructor at the class meeting on November 5.

An illustrative GIG was presented in Figure 3. Note that the overall design includes identification as a GIG, a title, the introduction, objectives, and the specification of the task and the product to be turned in.

Games and simulations can often be used to specify the task and product in a GIG. Some instructors develop their own games and simulations to fit the exact conditions and objectives of the course. Others select published games and simulations which fit their own objectives. Sometimes published games can be adapted to fit an existing course structure.

The GIG is an effective tool for guiding small-group activity within our model as well as in any instructional system where there is a desire to use small-group activity. When carefully prepared in relation to the unit objectives, it can be highly effective in helping students learn course concepts at higher cognitive levels.

Small-group work requires appropriate classroom facilities. Most colleges and universities have an abundance of classrooms with old style seats which are screwed to the floor. In such rooms, small-group activities can be carried on only with great difficulty. However, even in such a setting, students can be organized into a small group of three or four, if the seats are fairly close together.

The ideal room is one in which students are seated at tables. Banquet-sized tables afford an excellent arrangement for about six students working in a group. Student desks which have a table arm provide a second best approach to small-group work. They can easily be pulled into a circle.

Ideally, the room should be large enough to permit some distance between groups. However, groups can be quite close together. When all the students turn inward in a circle and speak across the circle, the volume is usually quite controlled and not disturbing to other groups.

The best length of session for small-group activities is in a class period, one and one-half hours long or longer. It takes some time for a group to study the task, select a chairperson and secretary, and get down to the task. It is also helpful to have access to coffee and/or soft drinks to make the work situation as comfortable as possible.

The evaluation of group work is typically carried out in one or more of three ways: (1) evaluation of the product, (2) observation of the group by the instructor or assistants while the group is at work, and/or (3) evaluation of their oral report if one is given at the end of the project. Evaluation is always on a pass-fail basis. After much experience in using letter grades or point values, it appears that pass-fail is the best approach. One of the chief problems which arises in group work is the differential competence and motivation of students to perform well and assume responsibility. Some work hard and/or have much to contribute. Others are less motivated and/or have weaker backgrounds. A uniform grade of C or 16 points to all members of a group often leads to severe problems of morale. The hard workers resent those who do little. The problem can be partially overcome by consulting with and offering guidance to weak students.

However, pass-fail grading seems to offer the best solution as far as morale is concerned. There seems to be less at stake. Grades in the course are based on other performances. If the students have turned in a project report or created some other product, it is evaluated carefully. If it is not completed satisfactorily, the group will be asked to go back to work. They must continue until the job is done satisfactorily.

The second mode of evaluation is carried out by the instructor as he/she circulates among the groups while they are at work. Here it is possible to evaluate both the overall progress of the group toward the goal specified in the GIG and the contributions of individual students. The instructor and/or the teaching assistants should spend most of their time, while students are working, sitting in with groups and fulfilling a helping and guiding role. If a group appears to be going wrong in some way, the instructor will intervene and try to help the group clarify the task. In such exchanges, he/she has the additional opportunity to observe how the group functions and reacts to guidance.

The third mode of evaluation is the evaluation of oral group reports at the end of projects. In graduate classes, an oral report is often required at the end of a group project. This usually includes the presentation of an outline or set of ideas written on a chalkboard or overhead transparency. This presentation of the group report facilitates evaluation of the overall group effort as well as evaluation of the chairperson (student) who presents the report.

The three modes of evaluation can be useful to instructors in providing feedback to students and in guiding future work.

The organization and composition of groups present some minor problems. In some units, the nature of the group task makes it desirable to group students according to a common interest or background. This would also be a function of the course and the nature of the students who typically enroll. In a nursing course, all students are likely to have a common background and common goals so that selective grouping may not be necessary. Conversely, in an education course, where students are preparing for diverse teaching majors, grouping may be quite desirable or even necessary. The problem for the instructor may be confounded by the variations in the composition of the class from semester to semester. There might be six students who are majors in English one semester, and only one the next. When there are six who have something in common, grouping is no problem. When there is only one, that student might have to be grouped with social studies and/or art majors.

If problems are anticipated in grouping students in a course, it might be desirable to avoid group tasks which call for group members to have common backgrounds. Certainly, much can be said for the merits of group projects in which students from diverse backgrounds work together and enrich one another's educational experiences through the interaction of the group activity.

It is a desirable goal in many courses of instruction to give students experience in group leadership and in working in groups. In most small-group instructional activity, there are two leadership roles, chair and secretarial. In the three-stage model, students rotate in the leadership and the secretarial roles from unit to unit. Some guidance is also offered at the beginning of each semester on how to lead a small group in projects. The small-group setting affords students an excellent, non-threatening setting in which to practice and later observe leadership behavior. Since many students are preparing for occupations in which they may begin in or rise to leadership roles, training in leadership behavior seems to be particularly appropriate.

Designing PIPs. The third stage activity is guided by the document called "procedures for individual projects" or "PIP." Like the SIG and the GIG, the PIP is typically a one-page document which builds chiefly upon the GIG in order to provide students with an opportunity to apply what they are learning to realistic professional problems, projects, or activities.

The document for a PIP, illustrated in Figure 4, is headed PIP and given the same unit title as the SIG and GIG. It begins with an introduction which builds upon the SIG and GIG and points the way to an individualized activity involving some professional or realistic application. Here is the introduction for a unit on behavior modification:

> You have learned the basic concepts and principles underlying behavior modification (BM) and especially have seen the links to Skinner's operant conditioning. In the group project, you had a chance to design a BM system. Now we want you to develop a specific plan for a behavior modification approach to a discipline problem which might confront you in your own classroom. Here you will learn how to design a BM approach to a specific problem child in your own classroom.

The PIP then states the behavioral objectives for this part of the unit. For the unit on BM, the objectives might be as follows:

(1) identify target behaviors;

(2) assess base rates for the behavior; and

(3) design a BM approach to the problem and specify exact teacher actions and materials required.

The task and product in a PIP should not be a simple repetition of the task and product assigned in the GIG. Ideally, it should involve the student in a synthesis activity in which principles and concepts learned in stage one are combined in ways suggested in stage two to create a relatively new product. Here is an illustration for the unit on behavior modification:

> Think of a behavior or discipline problem with which you were confronted in your own class or one you have observed in a classroom. Describe the problem in as precise behavioral terms as possible. Then think of a way to establish entry level base rates for the problem behavior.

> Finally, suggest a plan for manipulating the contingencies
> of reinforcement and eliciting desirable behavior. How will
> you assess the success or failure of your approach?

PIP projects are usually evaluated on a letter grade or point value basis. However, it seems desirable to use a mastery approach which permits students to do further work on projects which are grossly deficient in some way. Since the goal in PIPs is realistic or professional application, students should complete a unit with a good knowledge of how to *use* concepts and principles they have learned.

Closure and Internalization Activities. In closing a unit, some efforts should be made to achieve closure and internalization of things learned in the unit. It is often also desirable to get some student attitudinal evaluation of the unit. This might be achieved with a short summary presentation or lecture by the instructor and a discussion with the students. The goal should be to "pull ideas together" and to get students to view what has been learned as having intrinsic personal value.

A sample instrument used to achieve closure, internalization, and unit evaluation is presented in Appendix E. It might be best to have students complete it outside of class and bring it in for a brief discussion. It should provide the instructor with valuable information for evaluation of the unit.

Selecting and Training TAs. There is undoubtedly more work required in designing and managing a course in the three-stage model than in traditional instruction. Thus, plans should be made to provide additional assistance for the instructor. The best way in most colleges and universities is through a system of graduate and undergraduate course assistants. However, either type of assistant alone can provide the necessary help. A detailed description of the selection, training, and management of course assistants in the Purdue Three-Stage Model for the design of college courses has been presented by Linden, Ames, and Feldhusen (1977).

Undergraduate assistants are selected from previous classes in a manner analogous to an honors program. The best students finishing a course are chosen and invited to apply for positions as undergraduate teaching assistants the next semester. If accepted, the student enrolls for two or three academic credits. Some students repeat the experience more than one semester.

Graduate students in our own field, educational psychology, are typically required to spend at least one semester as unpaid teaching assistants in a course of instruction prior to being considered for placement as paid teaching assistants. Thus, they also constitute a pool of potential assistants for courses operating in the three-stage model.

Each of the graduate and undergraduate teaching assistants is assigned to a specific class or division of a course. A given class may have one or two of each. At the beginning of the semester, they participate in a day-long orientation session. As preparation for the orientation, they are required to read an article which introduces them to the three-stage model (Feldhusen, Ames, and Linden, 1974). Following the orientation, the TAs meet each week throughout the semester to discuss plans for the week's activities.

During class meetings, the TAs assist with test administration and group activities. Outside of class, they meet with students and participate in developing new units, preparing instructional materials, and other course management activities.

The experience as a TA is viewed as a learning activity. While TAs provide valuable help, they should not be looked upon as "slave labor" and relegated to the mimeo machine and collation jobs. Most of the undergraduate TAs view the experience as a valuable part of their education. For the graduate students, it is seen as a step on the way to college teaching. For the instructor, TAs are valuable assistants in conducting the course.

Recordkeeping and Grading. There are several other problems in designing courses in the three-stage model which must be considered. One is recordkeeping. Recordkeeping is somewhat more complicated in the three-stage model because of the frequent mastery testing or reaction papers and the grading of projects. It is also desirable to use a midterm and a final examination for summative evaluation of students' overall learning in the course. Thus, there is much information to be recorded and used in the evaluation process.

In addition to the records maintained by instructors, students are given individual mastery record sheets for keeping a record of their own performance. This record can be translated into a projection of the final grade at any point in time during the semester.

Grading also presents some special problems in the three-stage model. Since grading is mastery-based for all tests and projects except the midterm and final examination, all students can earn a satisfactory grade in the course. However, the grade level for mastery can be set at the instructor's discretion. It should probably be at least at a C level in undergraduate courses and B in graduate courses.

The final examination can be used in several ways in calculating the final grade. One way is to use it as a criterion-referenced measure with specified cutting levels for grades of A, B, C, D, and F. As a summative measure, it can be used as the sole criterion for the final grade or averaged in as a part of the final grade, usually one-third or one-fourth. Finally, the final exam grade can be used simply as a confirming grade. If the student earns a grade on the final of C or better, he/she receives a final grade determined by all other aspects of performance in the course.

It seems desirable to use a final summative examination to assess students' overall performance in the course both for individual student evaluation and for course evaluation. It also affords some index of how well information from course units is retained and transferred to the end of the course.

The Course Syllabus and Outline. The course syllabus and outline must also be given special consideration in the three-stage model. These two documents provide overall orientation and guidance for students. It should be noted immediately that merely giving these documents to students will by no means assure that they are read. Some instructors assign the syllabus as a reading and even quiz students on it. It is possible to have students read it at a first class session and to have the instructor point out especially important information in the document.

The syllabus should describe the operational use of the SIG, GIG, and PIP from a student's point of view. Here, for example, is the presentation concerning a SIG:

> At the beginning of each unit in this course, you will be given a one-page document called a "self-instructional guide" or SIG. The main purpose of the SIG is to guide your reading and study to acquire basic ideas for the unit. You should read it carefully as soon as you receive it. It gives you a brief introduction to the unit, states objectives which clarify what you are to learn, tells you what to read and study, and offers some self-quiz questions to check your own learning. You should find the objectives especially helpful, since they state what you should be able to do after doing the reading and study material.

The syllabus should also offer advice concerning the "group instructional guide" or GIG. Here is an illustration:

> In most of the units in this course, you will do a group project to help you understand the material better. This activity will be guided by a one-page document called a "group instructional guide" or GIG. It gives you a brief overview of the group project, presents the learning objectives, and states exactly what you and your group are to do, and what you are to produce in the way of a report. Your instructor will organize students into small groups for this activity.

Finally, the syllabus also presents some information about the "procedures for individual projects" or PIP. The following is an example:

> In most units in this course, you will also do an individual
> project. The individual project gives you a chance to learn
> how to apply ideas you are learning to specific problems of
> interest to you. You will receive a one-page guide called
> "procedures for individual projects" or PIP. It will give a
> brief introduction, state objectives, and tell you exactly
> what you are to do. You should plan to confer with your
> instructor after you decide on a project to make sure that it
> is suitable for the requirements of the PIP.

The syllabus should also discuss the nature and use of
instructional objectives from a student's point of view. In the
same context, testing and grading practices should be
clarified and the relationship to the objectives should be
explicated. Students should be told how to use the objectives
as guides in reading and studying and in preparation for tests.

The sequence and timing of course activities, especially
within a unit, need some initial explanation. Students need
help in keeping track of the sequence and interrelationships
among SIG, GIG, and PIP activities. They should also be
given guidance concerning how to organize course materials
in a looseleaf notebook. It is a good idea to punch notebook
holes in all materials distributed to students to help them in
organizing a notebook.

Two other topics which should be discussed are attendance
requirements and the roles of the instructor and the TAs. In
the three-stage model, it is best to have an attendance policy
which requires students to attend all class sessions. Optional
attendance is a problem in the three-stage model, especially
during group work. The complexity of general course
activities also demands that students be present in order to be
sure that they maintain contact with all aspects of course
activities. The roles of the instructor and TAs should be
clarified in order to be sure that they become maximally
helpful to students.

Finally, the instructor should clarify briefly his/her teaching philosophy. This might consist of one or several para-

graphs setting forth his/her views about teaching and learning. He/she might also wish to discuss here his/her views of student and instructor responsibilities.

The course outline is also an important document to give the student a general orientation. The course outline should present *specific* information concerning course activities. An illustration of an outline is given in Figure 7. The major features of the outline are the list of dates, the unit topics associated with those dates, the class activities, the listing of assignments due, test dates, and handouts. The outline provides a schedule for the instructor and the students. It offers some assurance of balanced coverage of course topics, and it provides motivation and guidance to students. The outline need not be an inflexible instrument dictating activities when a change in schedule might be desirable. However, it should provide the desirable pacing through the complexities of the three-stage course model.

The orientation of students in a course designed within the three-stage model depends upon several things, notably the syllabus and the outline. In addition to these documents, the instructor should discuss the course organization at the beginning of the semester and answer student questions about it. While the course is in progress, the instructor should provide continuing orientation and guidance in order to make sure that students understand the goals and the general procedures. As noted earlier, there is a special need to assist students in using and filing the various documents associated with the model.

The Roles of Instructors and TAs. The instructor of a course taught in the three-stage model plays a substantial role as course developer in planning units and designing the necessary instructional material. Since courses designed within the three-stage model are also somewhat more complex than typical courses, the instructor's role as manager or orchestrator is also substantial. In stage-two group activities,

Figure 7

Outline for a Course on College Teaching
Taught in the Three-Stage Model

Date	Topic	Activity in Class	Assignment Due	Handouts
Jan. 14	Introduction	GIG-Values		SIG-Goals Syllabus Outline Task no. 1 Paper on Three-Stage Model
21	Goals	GIG-Goals	Reaction paper	SIG-Objectives PIP-Goals
28	Objectives	GIG-Objectives	PIP-Goals	SIG-Characteristics PIP-Objectives
Feb. 4	Student Characteristics	GIG-Characteristics	Reaction paper PIP-Objectives	SIG-Learning theory PIP-Characteristics
11	Learning theory	GIG-Learning theory	Reaction paper PIP-Characteristics	PIP-Learning theory
18	Instructional principles	GIG-Instructional principles	PIP-Learning theory	SIG-Individualizing instruction
25	Individualizing instruction	GIG-Designing instruction	Reaction paper	SIG-Materials PIP-Individualizing
Mar. 3	Instructional materials	GIG-Teaching materials	Reaction paper PIP-Individualizing	SIG-AV Aids-I PIP-Materials
17	Audio-Visual Aids-I	Visitor	Reaction paper PIP-Materials	SIG-AV Aids-II PIP-AV Aids-I
24	Audio-Visual Aids-II	Visitor CAI & CMI	Reaction paper PIP-AV Aids-I	SIG-Microteaching PIP-AV Aids-II
31	Microteaching	Microteaching taping and viewing	PIP-AV Aids-II	SIG-Testing
Apr. 7	Testing	GIG-Testing	Reaction paper	SIG-Evaluating teaching PIP-Testing
14	Evaluating teaching	GIG-Evaluating teaching	Reaction paper PIP-Testing	PIP-Evaluating teaching
21	Test scoring & feedback	Visitor	PIP-Evaluating teaching	
28	Orchestration	Closure activities		

the instructor must become a group dynamics coordinator. In stage three, he/she consults with individual students as they carry out their projects. The instructor is, finally, a trainer of the graduate and undergraduate teaching assistants who work with him/her.

The TAs have several roles. Graduate TAs are expected to exert more leadership than undergraduates. They might take the initiative in developing new units, in developing tests, and in scoring tests and grading projects. Undergraduate TAs may participate in all these activities, but they rarely take the lead.

Summary. The design of courses in the Purdue Three-Stage Model requires attention to the topics which have been discussed in this chapter. The first stage of the process is to formulate goals. Then unit topics can be identified. When a first unit has been planned, work can begin on the SIG, GIG, and PIP. Each requires skill in writing instructional objectives.

In the initial stages of course design, it might be desirable to develop a flowchart of tasks and deadlines for the various plans and materials needed. This might be a good job for one of the TAs. The combination of operational demands of the course and the requirements of developmental tasks can be perplexing unless a clear, visible plan is available.

References

Ausubel, D.P. *Educational Psychology: A Cognitive View.* New York: Holt, Rinehart, and Winston, 1968.

Bloom, B.S. *et al. Taxonomy of Educational Objectives, Handbook I: Cognitive Domain.* New York: Longman, Inc., 1956.

Feldhusen, J.F., Ames, R.E., and Linden, K.W. Designing Instruction to Achieve Higher Level Goals and Objectives. *Educational Technology,* 1974, *14*(10), 21-23.

Kryspin, W.J., and Feldhusen, J.F. *Developing Classroom Tests.* Minneapolis: Burgess Publishing Company, 1974, p. 163.

Linden, K.W., Ames, R.E., and Feldhusen, J.F. Undergraduate Course Assistants as an Integral Factor in an Educational Psychology Course. *Teaching of Psychology,* 1977, *4*(4), 182-185.

Mager, R.F. *Goal Analysis.* Belmont, California: Fearon, 1972.

Santogrossi, D.A., and Roberts, M.C. Student Variables Related to Rates of Pacing in Self-Paced Instruction. *Teaching of Psychology,* 1978, *5,* 30-33.

Silberman, C.E. *Crisis in the Classroom.* New York: Random House, 1970.

IV.

OUTCOMES

The Purdue Three-Stage Model for the design of courses stresses goals which lead to broader and more meaningful learning. Many courses promote only the simplest kind of learning of bits and pieces of information. While the stated goals may often be quite lofty, the actual learning might best be represented by the disconnected multiple-choice test items which are classifiable at levels one and two of the Bloom *et al. Taxonomy* (1956).

The following goals have been formulated for an undergraduate educational psychology course taught at Purdue University:

(1) learn a set of basic concepts, principles, and theories;

(2) become self-directed learners;

(3) develop higher cognitive abilities;

(4) learn how to apply knowledge to realistic professional problems;

(5) develop competence in working with others on professional problems;

(6) learn to help one another achieve course goals;

(7) achieve personal relevance from the course experiences; and

(8) appreciate the course as a model of instructional design.

Each goal will be discussed briefly as an outcome of the course. In addition, the following topics will be discussed:

(9) benefits to the TAs; and

(10) advantages for the instructor.

Students Learn Basic Concepts. The first goal of courses taught in the three-stage model should be to have students learn a set of basic concepts, principles, and theories in the discipline represented by the course. Stage one of the model, and specifically the self-instructional guide along with mastery testing, are addressed to this goal. The final examination procedures, discussed earlier, also reinforce this goal and provide further evaluation of its attainment. For the most part, it is achieved through directed reading. Because of the pacing and the mastery testing, students are quite likely to keep up on their reading and study and not resort to cramming. The learning of basic concepts, principles, and theories is prerequisite to most of the subsequent work in stages two and three. From the results of the mastery tests, student work in stages two and three, and the final examination, it appears that student achievement of basic information is quite adequate in courses we have taught at Purdue.

Becoming Self-Directed Learners. The second goal or outcome is achieved through stages one and three. In stage one, students must carry on the instructional activity of learning basic information on their own. In stage three, they work independently on applied projects. Both experiences should contribute to student growth in skill in directing themselves as learners. The stage one learning experience is closely similar to the procedures used in the Personalized System of Instruction (PSI) (Keller, 1968).

Developing Higher Cognitive Abilities. The objectives for stages two and three and the correlated learning activities are all designed at the higher levels of the Bloom *et al. Taxonomy* (1956). Furthermore, the activities are directed to application of new learning in realistic or professional settings. Most of the group and individual projects involve objectives at the levels of analysis, synthesis, and evaluation of the *Taxonomy.* Thus, student learning in stage three should transcend the typical stage one learning of pieces of information which characterize so much teaching.

Learning How to Apply Knowledge. The task of learning how to apply new knowledge to real professional problems is rarely addressed in teaching. Most instructors settle for rote learning of basic information. In the Purdue Three-Stage Model, as implemented in courses which have some relevance to professional activity, the group activity in stage two and the individual projects in stage three are directed to real professional applications in most units. Often this means simulated problems and paper-and-pencil products as the solutions. However, the projects are designed as realistic applications and provide experience to achieve this goal.

Competence in Group Work. Professionals in most fields have to learn how to work with peers and to lead their peers in projects involving professional tasks and problems. The group activities of stage two of the model promote experience both in working in a group and in leading a group who are working on professional tasks. Instructors are also urged to provide guidelines to students on how to work effectively in a group and on how to lead a group working on an intellectual task.

The instructor and TAs circulate and observe group activities in progress and also offer additional guidance, as necessary, to help groups learn to function effectively. Overall, the experience in group work is a valuable one for students enrolled in courses taught by the three-stage model. Instructors also have a need to learn how best to assist students in achieving this goal. The faculty and TAs conducting a course in the three-stage model should spend some time discussing methods for helping students to develop competence in group work.

Helping One Another. Many courses of instruction are taught in a manner which breeds excessive competition. Norm-referenced testing also tends to create strong competition among students. In the three-stage model, students are urged to study cooperatively in stage one to prepare for the mastery tests. The stage two cooperation is obviously a necessity, and it is promoted by instructors. It seems likely that this goal is being achieved in courses taught in the model.

Achieving Personal Relevance. The battle cry among students in the late 60's and early 70's seemed to be relevance of courses, but defining relevance often was quite difficult. Frequently, it degenerated to personal interest or whim. In any event, relevance is certainly a matter of perception. An alternative view of relevance stresses the knowledge and experience of instructors in specifying desirable learning goals for students. The latter characterizes the starting point in the three-stage model. The information taught in stage one and the projects in stages two and three should be selected on the basis of relevance to on-the-job problems in professionally oriented courses. Hopefully, if properly selected, students will perceive the relevance. Instructors should also tell students about the potential relationship of course activities to on-the-job experiences so that they will more readily discern the relevance of course activities. Most instructors at Purdue have found that students generally view the course content and activities as highly relevant to the occupation for which they are preparing.

Appreciate the Model. Students should perceive the design of a course taught by the three-stage model as an integrated approach with significant components for the production of learning. The components trace to well-established theory and design of instruction. Students are urged to become aware of the model and its elements. A short paper handed out at the beginning of the course introduces the model. The experiences throughout the course reinforce this learning. While it is not proffered as the ultimate or ideal model, it is suggested that it is a carefully thought out integration of educational concepts. Students should come to see it as a systematic instructional model.

Benefits to TAs. A description of how teaching assistants can and should be used in teaching courses in the three-stage model was given earlier. Aside from the assistance they provide to the instructor, a major goal is to provide experiences in course design and teaching to students who are in teacher education programs at both the graduate and undergraduate levels. The experience is a carefully guided one, not an *ad hoc* experience. It begins with an orientation workshop at the beginning of the semester and continues in weekly meetings in which course operations are discussed and new units are planned. The TAs are involved in discussing all issues relating to ongoing operations and course development. They work closely with the instructor, and they also work directly with students. Thus, they learn a great deal about course design and management.

Instructor Benefits. Courses developed and taught in the three-stage model require some extra effort in the development stage, but once in operation, the instructor's task may be less demanding than in traditional courses. There is little need to prepare and give lectures. Course materials are usable from semester to semester. The course becomes a replicable system which, to a great extent, can be activated by TAs and secretaries. The instructor must, of course, be the overriding course manager, and his/her various roles have been described. However, the instructor's presence at all meetings is not so essential as it is in the lecture course. The TAs can handle the group sessions occasionally. The TAs can also help a great deal with test scoring, paper grading, and recordkeeping.

The model also affords an excellent setting for several kinds of instructional research activities. Data on student performance can be gathered in relation to various aspects of course activity. New instructional components can be evaluated experimentally. For the lead instructor who may have limited time for empirical research in other areas of basic interest, the course can provide a data base which, in turn, can and should lead to productive research publication.

Finally, it should be noted that courses taught in the three-stage model constitute a specifiable curriculum. The goals and objectives are readily available to instructors of other courses who wish to know what was taught in the course. It is proverbial on college and university campuses and in high schools that every course is idiosyncratic in content to the instructor teaching the course. In a three-stage model course taught by several different instructors, the learning outcomes are readily identified.

References

Bloom, B.S. *et al. Taxonomy of Educational Objectives, Handbook I: Cognitive Domain.* New York: Longman, Inc., 1956.

Keller, F.S. Goodbye, Teacher . . . *Journal of Applied Behavior Analysis,* 1968, *1,* 78-89.

V.

DEVELOPMENTAL GUIDE

The initial work in developing the three-stage model began with several kinds of exploratory teaching activities. Small-group approaches were explored for several years along with the support of graduate and undergraduate TAs. Several instructors had tried mastery testing, and several kinds of support documents had been developed which later became SIGs, GIGs, and PIPs. Finally, in 1972, a commitment was made to design and implement a new system for the undergraduate educational psychology course at Purdue University. It enrolls about 400-500 students per semester, and they are taught in groups of 35-40 students each.

The developmental process began with a two-day planning conference to formulate goals and a broad outline of the plan. This resulted in a specific plan which was implemented. Since that time, several other courses have been developed in the three-stage model at Purdue and at other colleges and universities. Over the several years of experience, the following guidelines have emerged as a working sequence for the development of a course in the Purdue Three-Stage Model.

1. Select the course. If several faculty are involved in teaching it, organize the team who will work on the project. Finally, select a chairperson or leader. If only one person is involved, he/she proceeds alone.

2. The team members, or the teacher working alone,

should read through this book to become familiar with all aspects of the design. The following chapter, on "Resources," should also be consulted for additional readings.

3. The team members, or the teacher alone, should have a lengthy planning meeting to plan the general direction of their or his/her developmental work, to select a team leader (if it is a team development), and to decide on how the model will be implemented. Developers should plan to adapt the model to their own situation. Some might elect to use only available books for SIG resources, while others might wish to develop minicourse self-instructional units.

4. Broad goals should be formulated and discussed, if the development is to be done by a team. Goals were discussed and illustrated earlier in this book. A set of goals should be written to represent the needs and unique characteristics of the course and students.

5. Develop plans for selection, recruitment, training, and supervision of TAs. Ideally, undergraduate TAs should be students who have taken the course and who performed very well. Graduate student TAs should spend at least one semester as apprentices learning the system before they become fully qualified TAs.

6. Develop a tentative outline of course units. This should be done by the team if a team is involved.

7. Prepare a SIG, GIG, and PIP for the first unit. Develop the course syllabus and outline.

8. Decide on the testing format to be used. Develop the mastery test, if it is so decided, for the first unit. Also develop plans for test administration and scoring procedures.

9. Consult with administrators concerning suitable rooms and course scheduling. Seek rooms with tables and chairs. A twice-a-week meeting arrangement, with each session one and one-half hours long, is ideal.

10. Plan for the orientation of TAs for the first unit.

11. Begin teaching the first unit while simultaneously

beginning development of the second unit. Plan for the organization of groups.

12. Develop plans for formative evaluation and discussion of the first unit with TAs.

13. Formulate plans for evaluation of GIG projects and PIP projects. Also make plans for recordkeeping.

14. Plan for closure and evaluation activities at the end of each unit.

15. Plan for the midterm and/or final examination.

16. Plan for course and instructor (and TA) evaluation with student rating forms at the end of the course.

17. Plan for a major review of problems and successes at the end of the quarter or semester by the instructional team.

18. Formulate plans for course revision and development during the next semester.

A PERT (Program Evaluation and Review Technique) charting of developmental tasks should be prepared for the first time through. The plan suggested above can be carried out with as little as a one-week head start on the semester or quarter. Thus, much of the developmental work goes on while the course is in progress with the developers staying a week or two ahead of the class. This provides an arrangement for obtaining and using formative feedback while the development work is in progress.

This developmental guide is, of course, highly condensed, and should be developed or elaborated with all the details discussed in previous chapters. Without such a plan and without close supervision by the project leader, the course development process might be jeopardized and schedules might not be kept.

VI.

RESOURCES

Three types of resources are available to instructors who wish to implement the Purdue Three-Stage Model in a course or courses. The first, and perhaps best, is to organize a workshop for the participating faculty and TAs. The author of this book and several of his colleagues are available to lead such workshops. Ideally, the workshop should be two or three days long. At a minimum, it must be one day in length. The workshop is conducted in the mode of the three-stage model.

The second type of resource is to have a consultant work with the developers. Again, the author and several of his colleagues are available to work with faculty who are implementing a course in the three-stage model. While these people would all have backgrounds in educational psychology, they have nevertheless had much experience in working with faculty from various disciplines in instructional development.

The third type of resource is printed information. A number of articles have appeared in books and journals discussing various aspects of the Purdue Three-Stage Model:

Ames, R.E., and Linden, K.W. *Small-Group Problem-Solving Activities for Applied Educational Psychology: A Three-Stage Model.* Prospect Heights, Illinois: Waveland Press, 1978.

Ames, R.E., Linden, K.W., and Feldhusen, J.F. Guided Group Problem-Solving in the Purdue Three-Stage Model of Instruction. *Educational Technology,* 1977, *17*(8), 12-16.

Feldhusen, J.F. The Effects of Small and Large Group Instruction on Learning of Subject Matter, Attitudes, and Interest. *The Journal of Psychology,* 1963, *55,* 357-362.

Feldhusen, J.F. Designing Instruction to Achieve Higher Level Goals and Objectives. In J.B. Maas and D.A. Kleiber (Eds.), *Directory of Teaching Innovations in Psychology.* Washington, D.C.: American Psychological Association, 1975, 421-422.

Feldhusen, J.F. Instructional Development. *Faculty Development and Evaluation in Higher Education,* 1977, *2*(4), 24-26.

Feldhusen, J.F. Issues in Teaching Undergraduate Educational Psychology Courses. In D.J. Treffinger, J.K. Davis, and R.E. Ripple (Eds.), *Handbook of Teaching Educational Psychology.* New York: Academic Press, 1977, 313-331.

Feldhusen, J.F., Ames, R.E., and Linden, K.W. The Purdue Three-Stage Model for a College Course. *APA Division 2 Newsletter,* October, 1973, 5-6.

Feldhusen, J.F., Ames, R.E., and Linden, K.W. Designing Instruction to Achieve Higher Level Goals and Objectives. *Educational Technology,* 1974, *14*(10), 21-23.

Feldhusen, J.F., Bodine, R.L., and Crowe, M.H. A Model of Instruction as the Base for Course and Instructor Evaluation. *College Student Journal,* 1976, *10*(3), 197-203.

Feldhusen, J.F., Linden, K.W., and Ames, R.E. Using Instructional Theory and Educational Technology in Designing College Courses. *Improving College and University Teaching Yearbook 1975.* Corvallis, Oregon: Oregon State University Press, 1975, 64-69.

Feldhusen, J.F., and Treffinger, D.J. Psychological Background and Rationale for Instructional Design. *Educational Technology,* 1971, *11*(10), 21-24.

Feldhusen, J.F., and Wang, H. Discussion Groups in Educational Psychology. *Journal of Teacher Education,* 1966, *17,* 83-88.

Linden, K.W., Ames, R.E., and Feldhusen, J.F. Undergraduate Course Assistants as an Integral Factor in an Educational Psychology Course. *Teaching of Psychology,* 1977, *4*(4), 182-185.

VII.

APPENDIX A

The Nature of Giftedness and Talent

Introduction

Almost any teacher meets students classified as "gifted." When the students are doing excellent work, placing them in the gifted category may not be hard. However, the teacher needs to know characteristics to watch for in order to be able to identify the potential for giftedness when it may not be obvious. This unit provides information concerning traits of the gifted. Consider, as you read, the effects of personality traits characteristic of the gifted on their academic lives and personal adjustment. Watch for research findings that contradict what you have formerly believed to be true.

Objectives

(1) To be able to list characteristics of the gifted.
(2) To be able to present a general description of the gifted or talented child.
(3) To be able to hypothesize specific problems the gifted may encounter.
(4) To be able to identify questions research has asked about and answered about the gifted.

Instructional Activities

Read the following and write a reaction paper to the ideas presented.
(a) Torrance, E.P. *et al. Creative Learning and Teaching,* 1970, Ch. 3.
(b) Gallagher, J.J. *Teaching the Gifted Child.* 1975, Ch. 2.
(c) Feldhusen, J.F. *et al.* The Right Kind of Programmed Instruction for the Gifted. *NSPI Journal,* March, 1969, 13, 6-9.

Supplementary Readings or Activities
(1) Make a brief list of persons you have encountered in literature who show characteristics of the gifted. List some traits. Do you consider their problems a result of their giftedness?
(2) Make a list of well-known achievers whose giftedness was apparent in childhood or adolescence.
(3) Check the newspaper daily for articles describing gifted children and adolescents.

Discussion Questions
(a) Are humans the only species that show giftedness?
(b) If you were the parent of a gifted child, would you feel there were special problems to avoid?
(c) Should a teacher be concerned about a gifted student who achieves at the level of an average student?

GIG
The Nature of Giftedness and Talent

Introduction
When a teacher is alert to characteristics of giftedness and recognizes traits common to the gifted among students in the classroom, he/she has made only a first step. The next step is to design teaching and classroom management plans to enhance the potential of the gifted and to avoid possible problems. The plans developed from year to year would probably vary to accommodate individual differences among the gifted.

Objectives
(1) To be able to identify characteristics of the gifted.
(2) To be able to clarify social adjustment problems of the gifted.
(3) To find possible techniques a teacher might use to aid gifted students in personal adjustment.

Group Activities
(a) What are major characteristics of the gifted people you have known?
(b) What characteristics, if any, bother you? Why?
(c) What characteristics bother other children? How?
(d) Should we learn to accept any of these characteristics? Which ones?
(e) Should we help the child overcome any of his/her characteristics? Which ones? Suggest ways we might do this.

Products
(1) Prepare brief written answers to the questions above.
(2) Be prepared to have someone in your group report orally on all or any of the topics.

PIP
The Nature of Giftedness and Talent

Introduction
Forming positive attitudes about the gifted is as important for a teacher as identifying the gifted and providing specifically for them in the classroom. Through positive attitudes, the teacher can help gifted children view themselves positively. The teacher must help them view their problems in perspective and learn to overcome these problems while also encouraging them to appreciate their abilities and take pleasure in using them. Ultimately, this task should be a pleasant one for the teacher.

Objectives
(1) To identify specific characteristics of the gifted in a person or pupil you have known.
(2) To isolate problems this gifted person has faced and his/her solutions.
(3) To specify those aspects of his/her personality and abilities that a teacher could help him/her learn to appreciate.

Product
Write a paper describing a gifted person or child you have known. (1) Cite problems the person has had, if any, that were due to his/her giftedness. (2) Describe the methods he/she used to cope with his/her problems. (3) Tell about his/her joys or satisfactions.

VIII.

APPENDIX B

Introduction
Broad goals must be translated into specific instructional objectives and/or educational activities. Instructional objectives are used in designing specific instructional activities related to the curriculum, discipline, or subject matter. Some goals are translated directly into course activities, not into objectives.

Our concern in this unit will be with the formulation of instructional objectives. We want you to learn how to write your own objectives, but we also want you to become aware that sets of objectives are now being published in many disciplines. Thus, it might be possible for you to select rather than write your own objectives.

Objectives
(1) To be able to write behavioral objectives.
(2) To be able to write objectives at all levels of the Bloom *Taxonomy*.
(3) To be able to write some affective objectives.
(4) To be able to write some psychomotor objectives (optional).
(5) To be able to formulate a set of objectives for a unit of instruction using a specification chart procedure.

Instructional Activities
Read from the following list and write reactions to or evaluations of the sources you use.
(1) Kibbler, R.J. *et al. Objectives for Instruction and Evaluation,* 1974.
(2) Mager, R. *Preparing Instructional Objectives,* 1975.
(3) Bloom, B. *et al. Taxonomy of Educational Objectives, Handbook I: Cognitive Domain,* 1956.

(4) Krathwohl, D.R. *et al. Taxonomy of Educational Objectives, Handbook II: Affective Domain*, 1964.
(5) Harrow, A.J. *A Taxonomy of the Psychomotor Domain*, 1972.
(6) Kryspin, W.J. *et al. Writing Behavioral Objectives*, 1974.

Instructional Objectives—
Self-Quiz
(1) What are the benefits of using behavioral objectives?
(2) What are the six levels of Bloom's *Taxonomy*? How do they differ?
(3) Are there cognitive components of the affective domain? Are there cognitive or affective components of the psychomotor domain? Explain.
(4) How do you determine when and where affective and psychomotor objectives are useful?
(5) How can behavioral objectives in the cognitive, affective, and psychomotor domains be applied to your teaching area?

GIG
Instructional Objectives

Introduction
Many of you will become models, resource persons, or consultants for others who are interested in instructional development. In those roles, you might have to teach others about instructional objectives. If you undertake such a task, you would certainly want to have your own instructional objectives for a unit on objectives clearly formulated.

Objectives
(1) To be able to work with others in selecting topics and preparing a sequential outline for a unit on instructional objectives.
(2) To be able to prepare a small specification chart for your unit.
(3) To be able to write some objectives for the unit at all levels of the Bloom *Taxonomy*.

Tasks and Products
(1) Prepare a specification chart of objectives for a unit on instructional objectives.
(2) Write your objectives in the order in which they would be taught on a transparency for display to the class. Show the taxonomy level for each objective.

PIP
Instructional Objectives

Introduction

Instructional objectives should be written or selected for all topics covered in a course. They should be specific enough to be useful to you in designing instructional activities and tests, and they should be useful to students as guides to learning. In some disciplines, complete sets of objectives have been published. In such cases, the instructor can merely select those which he/she believes appropriate for his/her courses.

Objectives
(1) To be able to write the behavioral objectives for a unit of instruction.
(2) To be able to write objectives at several levels of the Bloom *Taxonomy* or in the affective and psychomotor domains as well as the cognitive.
(3) To be able to use a specification chart approach to the organization of a set of objectives.

Tasks and Products
(1) Search for available sets of objectives in your discipline.
(2) Select a topic. Break it down into parts and arrange the parts into a sequential outline.
(3) Prepare a specification chart.
(4) Write or select objectives for cells as you feel necessary or appropriate.
(5) Write at least one or more affective objectives for the same topic.

IX.

APPENDIX C

SIG
Instructional Materials

Introduction

In this unit, we will examine the various approaches to the development of self-instructional materials. Self-instructional materials may consist of communications which chiefly serve to guide a student's efforts in learning, or they may consist of materials which in and of themselves do all or most of the job of teaching something. Our basic self-instructional device is identified by the acronym BOOK (Basic Organization Of Knowledge) and refers, to just that, a book. We will explore several other types of self-instructional materials. These materials are often used chiefly to teach objectives at levels one and two of the Bloom *Taxonomy,* but, in truth, all levels of the *Taxonomy* can be taught with self-instructional materials.

Objective

(1) To be able to identify the basic components of the following self-instructional materials:
(a) self-instructional guides
(b) group instructional guides
(c) procedures for individual projects
(d) self-instructional units
(e) audio-instructional units

Instructional Activities

Read three or more of the following and write a reaction paper.
(1) Johnson, R.B. *et al. Assuring Learning with Self-Instructional Packages,* 1973.
(2) Russell, J. *Modular Instruction,* 1974.

73

(3) Creager, J. *et al. The Use of Modules in College Biology Teaching,* 1971.
(4) Baker, R. *et al. Instructional Product Development,* 1971.
(5) Baker, R. *et al. Instructional Product Research,* 1971.
(6) Popham, W.J. *et al. Rules for the Development of Instructional Products,* 1967.

Instructional Materials—Self-Quiz
(1) Name the components of each of the five types of materials.
(2) What is distinctive about each type?
(3) Which type is most elaborate and time-consuming to develop?

Optional Activity
Identify and describe several other types of self-instructional materials.

GIG
Instructional Materials

Introduction
It is now well recognized that an essential element of instruction is the materials used in teaching, especially the printed media used to present information and guidance to students. Of course, other media, such as films, slides, and transparencies, also play vital roles in instruction. The development of good teaching materials should be a major goal of all teachers.

Objectives
(1) To be able to examine some available teaching materials and suggest ways to improve them to fit the needs of a particular subject matter area.
(2) To be able to suggest or design alternate forms of instructional materials to fit the demands of a subject matter area or the special characteristics of students in that area.

Tasks and Products
Focus your efforts on the SIG, GIG, PIP, and Minicourses as illustrated in this course. Then answer these questions:
(1) How would you modify or improve each to make them better for use in your subject matter area?
(2) Suggest or design alternative forms of instructional materials to fit your subject matter or your students.

PIP
Instructional Materials

Introduction

We can expect much more widespread use of a variety of self-instructional materials in teaching. Developed well and used properly, these materials can do a better job than our conventional textbooks in teaching basic subject matter. Almost all of these new kinds of material are based on explicitly stated objectives. However, a number of new textbooks also have objectives stated at the beginning of each chapter, and we are assured that the text is designed to facilitate student attainment of the objectives.

If we can depend more and more upon self-instructional materials to teach basic information, teachers should be able to devote more time and effort to higher level and more creative learning activities, such as simulation problems, group work, and project activity. The latter should be more directly related to the attainment of higher level objectives, such as problem-solving, analysis, and synthesis.

Objective

(1) To be able to develop and evaluate the following types of self-instructional materials:
(a) self-instructional guides
(b) group instructional guides
(c) procedures for individual projects
(d) self-instructional units
(e) audio-instructional units

Task and Products

You are to develop three or more of the five types of self-instructional materials. For each of the units, objectives must be stated. In designing these units, you should consider the following:
(1) Are the objectives clearly stated?
(2) Is the student given some orientation or overview?
(3) What motivational procedures will you use?
(4) Are the structure and sequence carefully organized?
(5) Is the student actively involved?
(6) How do you provide feedback to the student?
(7) How will you use the unit in relation to other aspects of teaching?
Try out the material in your own teaching, secure performance data and attitudinal reactions, and revise the materials as necessary.

Turn in the units, plus a narrative discussion of each, following the questions stated above and using data from the tryouts.

X.

APPENDIX D

SIG
Testing

Introduction

Classroom testing is a fact that faces all teachers at all levels of instruction. Testing of students over specified content areas is the single most widely used means of assessing cognitive outcomes of instruction. The tests come in a variety of forms, depending upon the individual teacher's needs and/or skill in test construction. The majority require some written responses from the student, whether it is marking a correct response out of five choices, writing a definition, or writing a long essay.

This unit on testing will enable us to look at the various forms of tests used and how to write items for them. In addition, we will look at the rationale behind various test forms and how each can be used to assess various levels of cognitive learning according to Bloom's *Taxonomy*.

Objectives

(1) To be able to list and give examples of different types of test items.
(2) To be able to write test items which measure learning at all levels of Bloom's *Taxonomy*.
(3) To be able to determine a match between stated objectives and test items which measure those objectives.
(4) To be able to distinguish between testing as a means of evaluation and testing as a means of grading.
(5) To be able to formulate a defensible rationale for the types of test items you would employ in evaluating learning in a class you teach.
(6) To be able to suggest ways of avoiding or remedying some common abuses of classroom testing.

Instructional Activities

Read three or more of the following and write a reaction paper.
(1) Mager, R. *Measuring Instructional Intent,* 1973.
(2) Gronlund, N. *Constructing Achievement Tests,* 1968, Ch. 1-5.
(3) Marshall, J. *et al. Classroom Test Construction,* 1971, Ch. 1-10.
(4) Marshall, J. *et al. Essentials of Testing,* 1972, Ch. 1-6.
(5) Blood, D.F. *et al. Educational Measurement and Evaluation,* 1972, Ch. 5.
(6) Kryspin, W.J. *et al. Developing Classroom Tests,* 1974.
(7) Anderson, R.C. *et al. Educational Psychology,* 1973, pp. 126-168.
(8) Gage, N.L. *et al. Educational Psychology,* 1975, pp. 790-813.

Testing—
Self-Quiz
(1) What are the advantages and disadvantages of different types of test items?
(2) Is it necessary or desirable to always measure learning at all levels of Bloom's *Taxonomy?* Explain.
(3) How are stated objectives useful when developing test items or procedures? Do stated objectives serve other purposes?
(4) Is there a difference between testing to evaluate and testing to grade? Explain.
(5) When and how can testing be nonproductive?

GIG
Testing

Introduction

All of us have taken a number of tests in various classrooms. All of us have also likely constructed a number of tests to measure learning or evaluate the progress of students we have taught. Throughout these processes, we have formed various opinions about tests and have probably made certain decisions about the proper use of tests.

The only reason most commonly given by teachers for using tests is that they evaluate students' progress. This is variously stated as "To see what students have learned," or "To find out what students don't know," or "To see who has difficulty with what," and so on. In all cases, the intent is clear—teachers want to know how students are doing in their courses of instruction. Teachers have a right to obtain that information, but they also have an obligation to utilize that information in ways that will benefit their students. All too often, tests are given over specified content areas, corrected, graded, and returned to students while regular instruction proceeds on to another content area.

And nothing is done about that content the student either made errors on or lacks completely. This is one common abuse of testing we have all experienced from one side of the desk or the other. There are others that are equally widespread. As college teachers, we have an obligation to critically examine tests and how we use them.

Objectives
(1) To be able to identify some common practices that are actually abuses of classroom testing procedures.
(2) To suggest remedies to correct or avoid those abuses.
(3) To be able to identify valid uses of classroom tests.
(4) To be able to list some guidelines for the proper use of classroom tests.

Tasks and Products
(1) Prepare a list of common abuses of tests in primary, secondary, or college classrooms.
(2) List a way of avoiding or remedying each abuse in the above list.
(3) Prepare a set of guidelines for the ethical use of tests in primary, secondary, or college classrooms. Include the use of tests as evaluation devices for planning instruction and/or remedial activities as well as the use of tests in determining grades.

PIP
Testing

Introduction
Classroom tests constructed by an individual teacher are one of the main means of evaluating student progress in a course of instruction. It is our responsibility as teachers to assure that the means are properly implemented in attaining the desired end results.

Objectives
(1) To be able to analyze previous ways you have used tests in terms of strengths and weaknesses.
(2) To be able to write test items that assess all levels of Bloom's *Taxonomy*.
(3) To be able to demonstrate a match between stated objectives and test items which measure those objectives.
(4) To be able to provide alternative learning activities for student weaknesses which become apparent through your testing procedures.

Tasks and Products

(1) Prepare a short (one-two pages) statement describing the kinds of tests you have given students, why you gave them, and how you used the results. Talk about the strengths and weaknesses you found in your tests and some indication of the evidence you used to determine strengths and weaknesses.

(2) For your own area of expertise or the subject you can teach, prepare a test over some specified content area. Include at least three types of test items. Indicate which level of Bloom's *Taxonomy, Cognitive Domain* is being assessed by each item. Be sure to include at least one item for all six levels.

(3) Using Mager's Objective/Item Checklist (in *Measuring Instructional Intent*), demonstrate a match between at least two of the above test items and objectives you would state beforehand.

(4) Suggest specific alternative learning activities for weaknesses which are apparent by non-mastery of test items on your test.

XI.

APPENDIX E

STAGE THREE–CLOSURE

Directions: Circle the letter of your choice and respond to questions.

1. How much did you learn from the readings and self-instructional things listed on the SIG?

    A. A great deal, accomplished objectives
    B. A moderate amount, but could have learned more
    C. Little or nothing

2. If you circled B or C for number (1), what failures in you or the material could be blamed?

3. How much did you learn from the group project (GIG)?

    A. A great deal, accomplished objectives
    B. A moderate amount, but could have learned more
    C. Little or nothing

4. If you circled B or C for number (3), what failures in you or the material could be blamed?

5. How much did you learn from the individual project (PIP)?

   A. A great deal, accomplished objectives
   B. A moderate amount, but could have learned more
   C. Little or nothing

6. If you circled B or C for number (5), what failures in you or the material could be blamed?

7. Which activity in this unit seems most related or connected to things you are learning in other courses?

8. Which activities in this unit *seem* most relevant or useful to you in your future role as a teacher, counselor, therapist, or school administrator?

9. In what ways, if any, have you clarified your views of yourself as a future teacher? Do you see your abilities, attitudes, or values in any new ways?

10. What remains unclear, unanswered, uncertain in the content of this unit?

JOHN F. FELDHUSEN is Professor of Education and Psychological Sciences and Director of the Office of Instructional Development in the School of Humanities, Social Science, and Education at Purdue University, West Lafayette, Indiana. He earned his BA, MS, and Ph.D. degrees at the University of Wisconsin. He is a Fellow of the American Psychological Association and a member of the American Educational Research Association, the National Council on Measurement in Education, and Phi Delta Kappa. He is a member of the Executive Board of the National Association for Gifted Children, on the Editorial Board of the *Gifted Child Quarterly,* and formerly Book Review Editor of the *NSPI Journal* (of the National Society for Performance and Instruction). Dr. Feldhusen is author or co-author of a number of books. The most recent titles are *Teaching Creative Thinking and Problem-Solving, Writing Behavioral Objectives, Developing Classroom Tests,* and *Analyzing Verbal Classroom Interaction.* He is also the author of over 150 articles and book reviews.